THE POWER of ONE

HOW GUARDIANS CAN SUCCESSFULLY TRANSITION THEIR FOSTER CHILD INTO THEIR NEW HOME

ANTONIO D. GRATE

ISBN: 978-1-7372246-0-0

Publishing By: DemiCo National, LLC

www.DemiCoNational.com

TABLE OF CONTENTS

FORWARD

I've read, watched, and listened to numerous inspirational and motivational books, movies, and speakers. However, after meeting Antonio Grate and hearing his story, he has become one of the greatest on my list!

My name is Dewayne Malone, the founder of The Rescue Me Project, which is an organization tailored to inspire and educate youth.

In my late teens and early twenties, I began to fall victim to the want for material things, cars, guns, drugs, jewelry, homes, and cash—material things that I desired but I had not yet earned. The street began to lure me into its clutches, and I began to find it easier to make fast cash on the street rather than to work for it. At the age of twenty-two, I found myself facing a prison sentence, and stripped of all the material things that my illegal activities had provided me.

I did not cry over the loss of things. I realized they were not important. It was my disobedience to the Lord, my sin, the disgrace I had brought upon my family name, and the grief that my actions had caused them that I was sorry for. It was for these reasons and many more that I cried out to the Lord in prayer, repenting of my sins and asking for forgiveness, and re-establishing my relationship with Him. My prayers were answered, and I felt the Lord's love and grace. Since then, I have released several videos, literature, albums, and I am currently venturing to schools, conferences, churches, and more to inspire and motivate others to prevent them from making the same mistakes that I have.

The Rescue Me Project's mission is uplifting and being a voice for others. By making a monumental impact on one person, that individual is more able to have a positive impact on the lives of others. Through this cause-and-effect process, the world can become a more hope-oriented place, increasing the overall life positivity of all individuals.

We are grateful for the outstanding success reports that we've received as a result of the services provided by The Rescue Me Project such as: reuniting families, addiction recoveries, grade elevations, overcoming depression, and more!

I had the honor of meeting Antonio in May 2015. From the moment I met Antonio I realized that he had a spirit like I had never encountered that was linked to a story like I had never heard. As I grew to know him as a colleague and a friend I realized the greatest element of his heart was his willingness to share his story without hesitation. He definitely has a story that the world needs to hear.

After learning of his childhood, and all of the obstacles that he encountered and had to overcome...I'm convinced he's a real life superhero! I believe this book is about to become the much wanted and needed blueprint for every person who feels broken!

I'm so excited to know that he has decided to write this book with the hopes of impacting the lives of others. I've seen and heard of a lot of heartbreaking situations, but I have never witnessed the strength, drive, and passion that Antonio has after hearing every obstacle and difficult situation he has faced!

Antonio's transparency offers a motivating, inspiring, and empowering message on how to strategically get over the hurt, disappointment, and anger that plague so many of us today. I highly recommend that you read this book! Your life will never be the same....

Thank you Antonio for your obedience to the gift that God has given you and for sharing it with us! Love you bro!

~Dewayne Malone

INTRODUCTION

Television shows never depicted it, and movies never chronicled it. For decades mainstream media presented a narrative that every American household functioned, coped, and responded to difficulties all the same as that of the household of Mike and Carol Brady. When children bickered, it was resolved in a matter of moments. When children had difficulties at school, it was resolved in a matter of moments. However, the difficulties that prompted the child's classroom outburst was never linked to an unstable household environment. Parents were never depicted to have any mental or emotional instabilities. Parents were shown as near superheroes.

Such narratives weren't quite challenged until 1974 on the classic show *Good Times*, when 10-year-old Penny went to live with Willona after being beaten, burned, and abandoned by her mother. It was at that moment that viewers saw the harsh realities of childhood abuse on their tv screens in a way that had never been shown before. Penny's mother, a single mother, abandoned her after citing she could not care for the child financially, emotionally, or physically. It was also in that moment that for the first time many viewers were introduced to foster or kinship care.

Viewers watched in shock as the character Willona battled transition complications as she and Penny attempted to adjust to their new way of living. Television executives rioted against such a raw storyline that they felt gave an unreal depiction of the American family.

However, the storyline was tragically befitting to tens of thousands of children in America. But you have to understand that it was only roughly fourteen years prior in 1960 when the state of Louisiana kicked 23,000 children out of welfare systems due to being children born out of wedlock. Ridiculous measures such as what occurred in Louisiana was occurring across the county which led to the Department of Health, Education, and Welfare implementing the Flemming Rule. The rule was named after DHEW Secretary Arthur Flemming, which stated that states could not ignore the needs of children living in unlivable or safe home environments.

Instead, states would have to either provide the needed services to make the home livable or remove the children to more suitable living arrangements while still continuing to provide financial support on behalf of the child. To help states meet the demands of the Flemming Rule, an amendment to the Social Security Act of 1961 created the component to support the children in the state's care. States then received federal matching funds for foster care payments made on behalf of children who were removed from unsuitable homes.

By 1962, the Public Welfare Amendments to the Social Security Act required state agencies to report to the court system families whose children were identified as candidates for removal. Within a year's time the number of children entering foster or kinship care increased significantly. However, the nation was not equipped or educated on the role or need of foster parents, much less meeting the needs of the children now living in homes unfamiliar to them.

While the government likely did all they could think of at that time to meet the financial needs of the children pulled from their homes, the emotional, spiritual, and social needs of the children were often times overlooked. This was not just occurring among African American families as first seen on television in *Good Times*. Much like the tv character of Punky on *Punky Brewster*, Caucasian children were also now adjusting to living with non-parental relatives, foster parents, or adoptive parents.

Punky, also abandoned by her parents struggled greatly to adjust to being in the home of her caretaker, Henry Warnimont. While state approved foster parents were given tools on how to support the children during the transition periods into foster homes, relatives who were stepping up to raise the children of other family members did not get such training.

As many tips as shows like *Good Times* and *Punky Brewster* may have given to foster or kinship parents, those television programs still never tackled some of the trauma that truly presents itself in such situations. In real life, foster children often times run away, become violent, experience depression, or even attempt suicide.

As a trauma survivor and a child reared in the foster and kinship systems, it is my desire to help other adults serving as foster parents, kinship parents, or even mentors gain the proper tools to helping the child now in their care successfully transition and adjust to the drastic changes. As I prepare to share my story with you, I will also share tips to helping a child transition into their new foster care living. Let's take this journey together. Let's begin.

CHAPTER ONE

The Eye of The Beholder

I'm a 1980s baby from the South Side of Chicago. I was born on March 1st, 1981 at Chicago's Cook County Hospital to parents that were never married and never remained "together" after my birth. The 80s in the inner city of Chicago or "The South Side" (*the ghetto*) was a significant time period in the lives of many middle class and low income African Americans.

Growing up in the ghetto of Chicago was risky business. It was filled with crime, killings, drugs, gangs, and prostitution. I grew up on 45th and Indiana (*the low end*) and I assure you it was no easy task. In comparison to living in the projects, many might consider my old neighborhood to be comparable to suburban living. Nevertheless, the infamous Robert Taylor Homes (*the projects*) were only about three blocks from where I lived. So, you tell me, how "suburban" could my neighborhood truly have been? Things were bad, sure, but they were not all bad.

Learning to live through the sounds of gunshots less than four feet away became a normal part of my everyday life. But flipping outside with my friends on old thrown out mattresses and playing football in old vacant parking lots was also just as normal. There were some days when the Chicago heat would be so bad that the fire department would come into our neighborhood to open the fire hydrant, allowing us to play in the streets as the water forcefully shot out several feet high and wide.

Not only was my city and neighborhood considered one of the most ruthless areas in the nation, but a major drug epidemic had begun to sweep through the inner city like a tornado that no one saw coming until it was too late—and yup, you guessed it; it hit my neighborhood and my family hard! It took no prisoners and showed no mercy. Not only did this epidemic eventually overtake my mom, but it swallowed my sister and my cousin along with it.

My father was around, but he wasn't too involved in my life. My mom and dad both say they had intentions to eventually get married during their time together, but they never made those intentions a reality. After I was born, they stayed together for about a year or so but my mom's group of friends changed and as a result, so did her "habits" but not in a good way. My dad decided that he wasn't willing to compromise, and my mom decided the same, so they went their separate ways and left me hanging in the balance.

I don't remember anyone other than my grandmother going to church on Sundays, and on her Sunday morning walks to the Baptist Church that held her loyalty, she would pass my father's apartment building. If he was outside, she would stop to talk to him for a while.

During one of their conversations my grandmother informed him about the toxic environment my mother had created for me. She shared her thoughts with him concerning what was best for me, and that entailed removing me from my mother's care. I was still an infant, but my dad showed up and rescued his baby boy. He then left me in the care of my aging grandparents. He had showed up when it mattered but it wasn't until I was five years old that I actually remember having an encounter with him. I was home with my grandparents, as usual, when I heard a knock at the door. My grandmother called my name followed by instructions to come to the front of the apartment because there was someone, she wanted me to meet. My dad was there sitting in a wooden chair.

My grandmother calmly stated the words, "say hi; this is your father."

I looked at him, said "hi," and then went back to my room. I was five years old with toys to play with and coloring books to color in. I was a busy little man. I didn't have anything to talk about with a stranger who carried the title of "a father," someone whom I knew absolutely nothing about. Fathers were what kids had on TV and I was no TV star, so I also had no "father" at least not in the ways that it truly mattered.

My dad lived on 47th and Martin Luther King Drive, which was close enough for him to walk to see me. So, when he did make the time, we would spend a few hours together at our regular hang out spot, McDonald's. I don't remember our conversations during those days but I do remember our time together being filled with me learning something from him.

Whether it was how to hold a Big Mac so that it wouldn't fall apart in my little hands, or just the general lesson that people make time for who and what they want to make time for. He also taught me the importance of manners and asking for what you want. And while most kids would relish in the thought of knowing they had a regular date at McDonald's I took pride in knowing that I was learning what it felt like to truly have a father. Knowing he and I would be together was special to me because, first of all, I was going to McDonald's to show that Big Mac who was boss, and secondly, over time I began to really see what it felt like to have a parent intentionally "choose" me.

Whether you are a foster parent, or even if you have taken in the child of a relative which is often called kinship care, it is important that you do not become so attached to your eyes. Because of my difficult circumstances with my mom, I found it exhilarating to think that my father chose me. However, I would have been forever devastated had he engaged with me in a way that would have made me think that he thought I should feel honored that he chose me. As foster parents, you cannot present yourself to the child as their last source of hope, salvation, and decency after you've judged or even felt remorse for their difficult past. It is up for them to feel or not feel honored to be in your home, but you should never allow yourself to develop that expectancy from the child.

Most children who have been raised in difficult or unhealthy living environments have their own perspective or view on life and their experiences.

It is important that you understand your perspective may vary from their perspective. That is okay. However, you cannot challenge the child to a battle of who's perspective is accurate or more important simply because the child "needs" you or you may have the child's best interest at heart.

Often the story the child is telling his or herself about their parents, home, or life is the only thing that is giving them peace. Children will rather blame themselves than blame their parents. While, I'm not saying you have to support the child in self-blame, it is important that you inform the child that their current situation is not a consequence of their own actions. It is also important that you do not take that moment to point blame at who you believe to be at fault. There is no need for you to position yourself to be the superhero to the child. Position yourself as an ally of the child and his or her parents.

As a new child enters your home you have to first and foremost understand that everything you will observe from the child will be a consequence of his or her previous home. You must keep that idea in your mental and emotional gauge so that you do not confuse your perspective with the child's perspective. Regardless of how much you may know about the child's past, there will always be somethings the child will not share with you. The child will never want to feel judged for his or her experiences.

The manner in which you view the child's experiences will determine how you engage with the child. It is of the greatest importance that you take time to ask the child of his or her view on the matters that led to them living in your home. Then you must find the areas of their perspective in which you can agree with. This will validate the child, and you'll likely become a figure to whom they feel safe to share more of their story. If the child views his mother as the best mom in the world, you must align with that belief. It will not serve you or the child to challenge his view. The child's healing is not based upon your viewing, but rather his or her own.

I can recall being at a young age and preparing to go to my cousin's swim party. It was slightly awkward because I didn't actually know her, but that fact was irrelevant to me because I had never been to a swim party—but that day I was going! As I exited my apartment building, I noticed a long black car sitting idly nearby. No one in my family owned a car except for my dad and he wasn't around much, so I was expecting us to take the CTA (an abbreviation for the

Chicago Transit Authority), or even something more familiar to me, like the bus.

As I entered into the back of the vehicle, I felt like a fish out of water, but the act of getting into the car was a welcome discomfort. After sitting down in the backseat, the driver instructed me to put my seat belt on. Although I knew what a seat belt was, I wasn't familiar with how it actually worked and apparently my ignorance was apparent because my aunt leaned over to assist me with the small but unfamiliar task.

Upon everyone being safely secured, it was finally time to drive off. As I sat in the backseat of this very spacious car, looking out of the window, I enjoyed the experience of every moment and every view. The more we drove, the more I noticed how drastically the scenery began to change. In my mind, we were entering into uncharted territory. As we got closer to our destination, my mind was truly blown; a life altering game changer for my future perspective.

Every house we passed not only had a front yard free of debris, but they also had plush green grass. In my young mind, people like me just didn't see things like that! I didn't know such a thing even existed. Why didn't anyone tell me? Why hadn't anyone shown this to me before? I was raised to believe that a front yard was supposed to consist of empty bottles, soda and beer cans, trash, cigarettes, drug needles, and empty drug baggies.

I never spoke to anyone about what I had seen, but this moment was my plot twist, and this image would be forever engraved in my mind. I thought I was going to a swimming party to have fun, but in reality, I took a short trip from my own reality to a new world of endless possibilities. My eyes had been opened and my perspective was forever changed. Prior to that day I would often find myself staring out of my second-floor apartment window, wondering if there was more to life than what I knew. Wondering if I was allowed to have better, if I was allowed to have more.

CHAPTER TWO

Words of Mass Destruction

Even though violence, drugs, and poverty was such common norms growing up in my neighborhood, we still were kids. We craved any moment that we could find that would give us the opportunity to be just normal kids playing, laughing, and running about.

I still remember the day my eyes *opened* as if it was just yesterday. It was a Saturday afternoon, and as always, my friends and I were looking for something to do. Ultimately, we decided to play a game of tackle football in one of the vacant lots in our neighborhood on the south side of Chicago. Tackle football wasn't really my thing; I was more of a tag football kind of guy. Nevertheless, I couldn't be *soft* in front of the guys. There was also an older girl who seemed to always be around, and I definitely couldn't be soft in front of her. After choosing our teams, the game began, and during the game, I vividly remember thinking, *just chill bro;*

make sure you put in a minimum amount of effort so you don't get hurt cause ain't nobody out here getting paid for this. I spoke to myself often as a kid. I didn't think there was anything wrong with talking to myself. To be honest, at that young age I had a strong ability to reason with myself and what was occurring around me. So, even when I felt that no one else could understand what I was saying, I always knew that it made sense to me.

I truly could not have cared less who won the game. I was just grateful when it was finally over. I felt lucky to have made it out in one piece without being hurt. As we were exiting the lot, everyone was walking and talking but I must have said something that didn't sit well with the older girl because her words were not only sharp and swift, but they cut deeper than any scar I could have sustained during our football game.

"That's why your mom is a crack head!" She yelled out to me. Immediately, I was stricken with pain as her words began to infiltrate my bloodstream, my mind, my heart, and my soul. It was something that I had never felt before; a feeling I wouldn't dare wish on my worst enemy. I tried to control my emotions, but my eyes began to well up and tears began to rush down my face. As I stood there, silently sobbing, I found that I couldn't walk, and I couldn't talk. I was absolutely paralyzed with pain, shame, and even guilt. All I could do was cry while my heart shattered into a million pieces.

I knew that I would never be the same. She tried to console me, but her apologies fell on stony ground, because at this point it was too late—the damage was already done, and oh what damage it was.

My worst nightmare was now my reality. My perspective had been tainted and the filter in which I saw my life—my family and my mother—had drastically changed. It was a heartbreaking moment, but it was also an eye opening one. I was forced to see the world and my situation for what it truly was. It was unbearably difficult, embarrassing, heartbreaking, disappointing, and sad. But it was my reality; my life.

I now had to wrestle with the fact that my mom struggled with drug addiction and I was angry about it. After being *"outed"* by this mean girl, I had gradually begun to put the pieces together about my mom. I no longer had questions as to why I spent most nights at my grandparents' house when my mom lived right across the street with my younger brother. And when I did stay the night at my mom's, it was strictly on the weekends. When I was a bit younger, I would always wonder why my mom had so many visiting friends.

Family card games and other family moments were accompanied by my intense hatred of seeing people go in and out of the bathroom for extended periods of time. What was supposed to be a good time was always ruined by her overpowering urge to have her own turn in the bathroom. I was annoyed and frustrated that something as common as a trip to the bathroom was no longer innocent in my little eyes.

Why wasn't time with me enough for her to fight that urge? This was my constant thought. After all, I only had her for the weekend anyway. Did I mention that she was also a social alcoholic? I'll never forget the night I was awakened by hostile voices; my mom aggressively cursing out and threatening her boyfriend. My heart began to frantically race, and I was genuinely terrified as I silently lay in shock under the covers in my bed. I nervously waited for her to act on those not-so-empty sounding threats. This behavior became a normal occurrence with her, so it only made sense that I became immune to it. I didn't like it, and I knew it wasn't okay, but if I wanted to see my mom, I had to learn to live with it—after all, they were just empty threats.

After the mean girl on the playground opened my eyes to so much disaster in my life, I became such an expert on identifying the signs of addiction, that I was also able to determine my sister and cousin were also both using drugs. This demon was all around me, and all I could do was watch. I felt so helpless.

I'm sure it was the Words of Mass Destruction that I heard on a playground that sent me into a downward spiral. After that moment, I hated the term crack head. I never wanted to hear that word again. Let me explain. When specific words have broken the soul of a person, they will feel that same hurt every time they hear those words, even if the words are not directed at them. Guardians must be so intentional of learning the child's past culture so they can at all costs avoid using the words, terminology, or descriptions that reminds the child of his/her devastating past.

If you have decided that your family will serve as a foster family, then you must establish a healthy culture for everyone in the home.

You will not just be the foster parent, but your children will be foster siblings. Everyone in the household must be a part of the mission of accountability and boundaries. You must begin establishing this culture before the first foster child arrives. Your home is no longer a typical home, and it cannot function as such. Your home is now a safe haven, and you must be intentional about establishing a safe space. Innocent words that may not be offensive to you, your spouse, or your children, may trigger your foster child.

We all have words that are as daggers to our ears. So, allow your family to create and post a list of Words of Mass Destruction that are not allowed in the home. Allow everyone to contribute, but this must be established and practiced before the foster child arrives. While this practice may not be perfected by the time a foster child arrives, it will be of much more significance for the practice to already be underway.

Once the foster child arrives, allow the child to add his or her list of Words of Mass Destruction. Then, it is important that no one inquiries of the reasons behind one another's listings; just agree. The reason is not important. Do not require an explanation behind the child's intolerance of certain words. The goal is to immediately show the child that he or she can establish a boundary in the new home. A child that may have never felt he or she has had a voice, may suddenly feel empowered by such an act from the foster family.

You will have to be very intentional with this practice, but done correctly, you will see great rewards. I must add that steering clear of the Words of Mass Destruction verbally is one thing, but you must hold your television computer, mobile devices, radio to the same standard as well. That means you have to monitor what you view or listen to as well. What service would it offer the child to not hear his foster family use the term crack head, but music blasts in the home everyday with the term in the lyrics? Sacrifice! It is about sacrifice, and everyone has to be on board meeting the needed sacrifices for the new addition to the home.

The fact of the matter is this practice will enhance any family and household unit whether a foster child is present or not. Often, guardian's first approach with a new foster child is to establish authority over the child or they will aim to create a happy environment. In the initial days of foster care, a child only cares about his/her safety. This should be addressed first and foremost.

Chapter Three

Identifying the Child's
Internal and External Triggers

I have learned that nothing in life says *I love you* quite like acceptance. When we accept the space in which someone sits in their journey or experience, we remove the pressure for them to be more healed than he or she may actually be. One of the greatest ways of total acceptance of one is by accepting their triggers. We all have triggers. I don't care if you were raised in a *Leave it to Beaver* type of household or a Lucious and Cookie Lyons type of household. We all have these little things called triggers that prompt or incite our fears. I don't believe that God created us to live in fear. I do not believe that fear is natural, hence the reason adults and children alike make such poor decisions when their fears are triggered.

There are two types of triggers that I would like to share with you. I believe that if you invest the time in to studying these triggers, you may actually gain knowledge of your foster child that he or she may not yet have of themselves.

Internal triggers are the thoughts, memories, or feelings that have the ability to change one's emotional health regardless of their mood.

External triggers are the people, places, things, situations that bring about negative or fearful emotions regardless of one's mood.

While we all have both internal and external triggers, we more often fall victim to the external triggers. It is of great importance that you learn your foster child's triggers.

This can only happen by communication or experience. No matter how much information you receive from a case worker or someone more familiar with the child's experiences, there is still so much more that you will not know. Unfortunately, you will learn many of the child's triggers after the child has been triggered. For this reason, it is important for you to keep a calm head when the child is triggered and may be lashing out. You must remain in control of the situation so that you can accurately measure and analyze what just occurred. It is certain that the child has been triggered, but do not allow the moment to pass you without using it as a teachable moment for yourself and the child. Try this situation out for example. Imagine a foster mom named Kim as she engages with her foster son Bryan.

"Bryan, may I come in?" Kim said knocking on Bryan's bedroom door. Bryan doesn't answer. Kim enters. "Are you alright? I thought we were having a great time dancing with the other kids. Did someone do something that upset you?"

"I don't want to dance anymore. It's stupid." Bryan said folding his arms across his chest. Kim sat next to him on the bed.

"That's fine. You seemed like you were having such a great time. You're a really great dancer too. You seemed like you were enjoying yourself until that last song came on the radio." Kim said softly. Bryan lowered his head. "You don't like that song?" She asked. Bryan shook his head.

"My Mom used to turn that song up loud on the radio so I couldn't hear her screaming when her boyfriend would beat her up." Bryan whispered.

"I'm sorry Bryan. I'm sorry that you have such painful memories with that song. I will let everyone know that you and I don't like that song! Do you have a song that you do like that makes you feel better?"

You will notice in this situation that Kim instantly realized that little Bryan was triggered by a song that brought back very painful memories. In a matter of seconds Bryan went from being the life of the party to remembering what he believed to be his painful reality. Kim exceled further by standing as an ally with Bryan by assuring him that his trigger will be respected. Yes, it would be ideal for Bryan to be able to find the same joy, happiness, and fun in such a great, awesome, and popular song.

However, that is not his reality. Your foster child will challenge every opportunity to communicate likely out of fear of judgement or fear of making his or her parent look poorly. When the child realizes that your inquiries are simply so that you can support the child, the lines of communication will increase.

I was seven years old, and all I wanted to do was be a kid. I hated that so much of my thoughts were on things that kids should not have to ever consider, so I just wanted to be a kid. You know, just hang with my friends without my little brother cramping my style. However, wherever I went; he wanted to tag along. But there my five-year-old brother was on the opposite side of the street yelling,

"I want to come with you! I want to come with you!"

But he was too young to be hanging out with me and my friends anyway, at least so I thought. So, I replied with an emphatic,

"No! Stay across the street! As a matter of fact, go back inside with Momma!" Many times, when older siblings begin taking on more mature responsibility for their younger siblings, things get complicated. Some older kids become bitter towards their younger siblings, even though its not the fault of the younger children.

When kids grow up in such dysfunction, they're no longer able to be just a kid. I was doing everything that I could to return to just the kid space. I didn't like wandering about my mother's crack addiction. I didn't like wandering where I would sleep at night. I didn't like wandering all the thoughts that come along with being raised by a mother who is known around town as a crack head and a father who just seldomly pops in. Some older children just simply want to be a kid without having to consider anything else. That is what I wanted. That is what I craved when I told my little brother to go back inside to Momma.

Apparently, my response wasn't good enough, or he didn't respect me as the authority figure I felt I had unwillingly become, because every time he yelled "I want to come with you," he moved a little closer to the street as my friends continued walking in the opposite direction. I was now forced to backtrack, but I was determined to make him understand that I meant business. He was determined to change my mind though, as he gradually eased his way from the sidewalk to standing between two parked cars.

As I watched him come closer and closer, I also noticed that he had now found his way a few steps past the curb. Before I knew it, the screeching sounds of tires from a black van had come to an abrupt stop. My brother's small body bounced from the front end of the van and landed onto the Indiana Street pavement. Immediately, fear, disbelief, and shock ran through my body as my mind told me to run. I didn't run toward my brother's now motionless body, but I ran to my grandparents' second floor apartment to tell them about the accident. I didn't have to say too much because even from inside they had heard what had happened. I remember telling them that CJ was lying in the street, but everything else following that moment was and is still a blur. As I looked out of my second-floor apartment window my emotions and my mind were racing, and naturally, fear, guilt and blame quickly began to consume me.

Eventually the ambulance arrived, and they quickly made their way through the now largely gathered crowd. With every passing second, I could only wish and hope that the little boy who just wanted to hang out with his big brother would be okay. I couldn't shake the guilt, the worry, and the trembles of fear as I watched my five-year-old brother lay motionless in the street.

I never went to visit my brother in the hospital. Not because I didn't want to, but simply because no one ever offered to take me. Maybe they thought I was too young to see my brother in an ICU bed. Maybe it never actually occurred to them that I needed to see him to know that he was still alive. Maybe they simply didn't care that seven-year-old me was being haunted and tormented by the guilt of knowing that ditching my brother to be with my friends was a big reason why he was lying in critical condition, fighting for his life. Maybe they blamed me too.

My grandfather was an avid reader of the *Chicago Sun Times* newspaper, so several days after the accident, I saw a picture of my brother's accident on the front page. Someone had captured a picture of the paramedics working on him as he appeared to lay lifeless in the street; an oxygen mask no bigger than his face, assisting him with his breathing. Remember, I hadn't run to him after the accident, I ran to get help, so this was the first "real" image of the accident that I'd seen.

Immediately, warm tears hiding behind my eyes began to stream down my face. I tried, but I couldn't get the image out of my head. The article stated that he was in critical condition fighting for his life and, of course, this only further fueled my guilt. After a few months in the hospital, he made a full recovery and returned home. No one in my family ever talked to me about the accident.

No one ever asked if I felt guilty. And no one cared to ease the worry I carried on my seven-year-old shoulders. I was happy that my brother had made a full recovery, but I had these other emotions that my young mind couldn't comprehend how to cope with. As I grew older, these thoughts and feelings remained with me, remained part of me, and remained engraved in me as I tried to live life as though they didn't exist. Guilt and self-condemnation would move forth with me for many years of my life.

CHAPTER FOUR
Establishing Boundaries

Only the strong and fortunate survive, at least that's what I've been told. How can it be that a young kid from the South Side of Chicago could be exposed to so many toxic situations, and yet still have a healthy frame of mind to want a better life than what the streets had to offer? All it took was a birthday party on the other side of town for me to realize that the pressures of my environment didn't have to produce what they expected me to become—another victim to the dangers of the South Side of Chicago. My physical reality was the "normal" sound of gunshots.

Playing with cap guns outside one day and the next day hearing my mother frantically scream my name because I was blissfully unaware that this time those weren't the sounds of a toy gun I was hearing. I was simply minding my own business as the sounds, "Pop! Pop! Pow!" rang out less than twelve feet away from me. Everyone around me began to scream and run but I didn't take cover because I thought my friends were playing yet another game. I was very young, and my reality allowed me to be blinded to the dangers around me. I could have easily been another statistic plastered on the front page of my grandfather's beloved *Chicago Sun Times* newspaper.

There were times when I felt so alive, so different, and so aware that I was allowed to want more than what I was being offered. But most of the time I felt like the world around me was sucking every inhaled breath right back out of me. I was grieving from the pressures of life, grieving from the pressures of my changed perspective, grieving for my desire to have more, grieving so much that I was also losing hope.

It's been said that "as long as you're living, trials and tribulations are certain." But at what point do those trials and tribulations ever stop coming? When does life decide that you've paid enough of a penance for a situation that you didn't ask to be born into? When does life simply decide that you've been weakened long enough, so now it's time to build you back up and make you strong?

I was the perfect example of an oxymoron. I walked around like a fearless lion through the dramatic scenes surrounding me on a daily basis but internally I was actually afraid. Afraid of being stuck, afraid of dying, afraid of living, afraid that I was changing and no one around me noticed a difference. Drama and chaos were a part of my everyday reality—how dare I think that I was actually good enough to want more than this? How dare I actually want to live a life that required and allowed peace?

Don't get me wrong, there were a few great memories that the 'hood had to offer; like playing tag outside or riding my bike around the neighborhood. Countless games and races with my friends for nothing more than bragging rights. I could never allow the laughs and good times make me forget where I was. Coming back outside to stolen bikes was as common as seeing my mother and a group of her friends sitting outside with bottles of liquor and blasting music. Be a child, but don't forget that being a careless or carefree child has consequences.

Events like walking into an apartment building with my friends to visit another friend as we were greeted by the smell of gunpowder from the bullets literally flying past our ears was weighing heavily on me mentally. Being so close to the chaos that you could see the sparks each time the gunman pulled the trigger had become another added layer to my already blurred perspective. I never spoke of these incidents to anyone because... why would I talk about another abnormal occurrence on the 4500 block of South Indiana on the South Side of Chicago?

After the smoke clears, you get up, dust yourself off, and do your best not to be robbed, jumped, killed, or fall prey to the toxicities of your everyday life. Realistically, there is only so much of a survivor's mentality that you can possess before you ultimately become selfish in a way. In my case, I had to do what I felt made me happy and what was best for me. For example, my mom and sister would periodically ask me for money because they knew that I was a saver even at a young age. Yet I would never give it to them because I believed they would use the money for drugs. And if

I gave it to them then I wouldn't have any for myself. I became selfish, but in a good way.

One thing that has been withheld from most children is the opportunity and freedom to establish clear and precise boundaries with those around them.

No one gave me permission to tell my mother and sister "no", but I had to give the permission to myself. Growing up in the horrific streets of Chicago, I only had limited boundaries that I could establish with others because no one respected the boundaries of others. People did as they wanted when they wanted, and to whoever they wanted.

I felt voiceless and powerless as a child. I had no power and I hated it. The most important gift that you can give a child, especially a foster child, is the freedom to establish boundaries without fear of consequence. A child that is entering your home from a chaotic life is likely feeling powerless and is seeking some way to feel in control. That is a natural human emotion, and you can either help the child find his or her control, or you can be the target of which that control is directed.

Boundaries are completely common when it comes to parental boundaries. Parents or guardians waste no time listing the lines the child or children are not to cross. However, children rarely every are asked or allowed to express the boundaries they need enforced so that they may feel safe or respected. In the previous chapter, we read of Kim and her foster son Bryan. After family dance night, Bryan ran away to his upstairs bedroom and slammed the door closed. Kim, aware that Bryan was upset followed him to check on him. She knocked on his bedroom door and asked if she could enter. However, Bryan did not respond. Yet, Kim still entered.

Now, I know that many of you are likely thinking that I'm going to far with this empathetic approach when it comes to a kid, but we must rid ourselves of this dismissive attitude when it comes to the human child. The human child is exactly like the human adult. We all crave honor and respect. So, while

I am not saying that Kim should have given up after Bryan did not invite her into this bedroom, I am saying that she shouldn't have asked if his answer or lack thereof didn't matter. Many children who enter foster care have never had their own bedroom. Some have never had their own bed. So, if the foster child has his or her own room, you must allow that room to be what they need it to be, home. The house will only become home if their bedroom becomes home first. Imagine for a moment if Kim had of just spoken to Bryan from the other side of the door. The child who likely feels they have no say so over their life will appreciate your willingness to accept their boundaries.

Unless you have a good reason to be worried for the child's safety, don't snoop through their room, diary or phone. If the child is generally responsible and reliable, invading their privacy without a solid motive sends the message that you don't trust them and could push them to become more secretive. Of course, if you're in any way concerned about the child's wellbeing, this rule doesn't apply.

Avoid sharing details about the child's personal life on social media or with extended family and friends. Not only is it embarrassing for them, it's also likely to deter them from telling you their secrets and feelings in the future. Earn the child's trust by showing them that you're an impenetrable fortress when it comes to their personal business. It is important that you understand the child's boundaries in social settings. Your friends and family are not the friends and family to the child.

If your foster child needs some time to assess a social situation before they're ready to join in, do your best to respect and support them.

Instead of forcing them to say hello to everyone as soon as you arrive at a birthday party, take them off to a quiet corner and chat about the decorations, games and food you can see. When they feel comfortable enough, they'll join in the festivities.

You should also avoid telling other partygoers that your child is "shy" or "needs time to warm up". If the child hears you, they could feel embarrassed or internalize those labels. The child will likely engage once he or she feels the situation is safe and accepting of who they are. You must respect this process. I cannot explain how important this next one is. Do not force the child to express physical affection with anyone.

Forcing a child to hug a relative or a family friend is one of the most common ways in which we disrespect their boundaries.

Uncle Joe might feel like he knows your child thanks to the wonders of social media, but to the child Uncle Joe is nothing but a scary stranger.

When faced with our children's hesitation, we often insist by saying, "Go on, don't be rude! Give Uncle Joe a hug." This unwittingly teaches our kids to ignore their instincts and internal alarms. Respecting their boundaries can help protect them against abuse or exploitation.

Instead of hugging or kissing, it should be perfectly fine if the child opts to greet adults with a smile, wave, handshake or high five. If Grandma accuses them of having bad manners because they won't kiss her, gently explain why you're trying to respect their choice. If your preferences to respect the child's preferences are not respected, you should leave the gathering or ask your guest to leave.

As adults we far too often impose our will on our children and force them to do things they don't want to do. While some of the obligations we force on them are necessary for their safety – such as wearing a coat in winter and buckling their seatbelt – others can unintentionally violate their boundaries and teach them that they don't have ownership of their bodies. Many of these patterns stem from a time when children were meant to be seen and not heard and to respect their elders above all else.

CHAPTER FIVE
Coping Skills

I had experienced things for the first time that many young black boys and men in Chicago would never experience. I felt different, I felt alive, I felt better. I could genuinely feel the change in me. But do you know what the definition of insanity is? It's repeating the same thing over and over and expecting different results. So, although, I had experienced these new things that were shifting my perspective on what was possible for someone like me, I had also gone back to my old way of living in my old neighborhood. I had returned back to my comfort zone, which was beginning to make me very uncomfortable.

I had gotten so used to pretending to be okay with my environment that as my vision became increasingly clearer, I also realized there was nothing okay about prostitutes regularly roaming the street. There was nothing normal about walking down the street and being harassed or randomly frisked by the police. There was nothing acceptable about how normal the smell of weed and smoke was that often filled the halls of my apartment building. The constant reminder that my mom was an addict was present each day because each day, I saw "pharmacists" in my neighborhood claiming their drug-ridden blocks. The street pharmacists were taking over and the screaming police sirens throughout the night often reminded me that their duty was always calling.

The drunks had taken over the front of the corner liquor stores and as abnormal as it was, I went on as if everything was well, fine, and good. But it wasn't. I hadn't asked to be born into this kind of life. I hadn't asked to be raised in this type of environment. Yet, at that time I was convinced that I had no other choices outside of being born into this life and dying in it.

Would things have been different had my mother not been addicted to drugs? Had my neighborhood not been so rough, would my perspective have been different? I had questions that were forcing me to change, and no one even cared enough to recognize it. I was disconnecting from the reality that I was born into and I was ready to take control of how the things in my own life were playing out. I couldn't control my mother being addicted to drugs. I also had to swallow the pill of knowing that my sister and cousin were also addicted to drugs. And I was embarrassed, to say the least.

Not only did my family consist of drug addicts, but I also had a cousin who had become so addicted to the street life that hearing the words "you have a collect call from" followed by the name of the jail he was in had become a normal occurrence. I knew what he was doing, but what could I do?

My environment had given me a front row seat to the effects of drugs on not only my community, but also on my family. Each time I saw two or more people go into a bathroom or bedroom, I was reminded that the ticket for my front row seat was purchased and was non-refundable.

Between secretly following my mom when she was supposed to be walking to the liquor store on 47th and Indiana because I knew she was really going to score a fix, and the pressure of the gravitational pull of my peers to partake in illegal activities; I truly wasn't ready when God decided that it was an appropriate time to allow the love of my life, my grandmother, to be diagnosed with breast cancer. My heart was already dealing with so many other heavy matters and this literally felt like too much to bear. I watched as the woman who had taken me in when my mother had chosen drugs over me began to lose her hair. I watched her weight drop almost overnight, and I watched the hospital become more of her home than her actual home had been.

I remember waking up to the sounds of her voice crying out in pain. I was so afraid that I could do nothing at all except lie in silence, hoping that someone, anyone other than me, would hear her and go to her aid. My grandmother was the one person, the only person, in my life that I knew loved me when no one else did. She was strong, sensitive, caring, and thoughtful—she was beautiful.

You know the neighborhood matriarch who you often see in the movies, baking homemade cakes for the church and taking care of the kids on the block? The one that everyone respects as a person and entrepreneur but also had a hustle selling candy on the side? That was my grandmother. She not only taught me to have an honest hustle (and bought my first pair of Jordans when sneakers with holes had become my norm), but she was also my first introduction to church.

She was a church nurse, so I knew that watching her get dressed in her all-white uniform, shoes, and gloves meant that it was time for church—and one Sunday I just had to go see what it was all about! Unfortunately, my young ears were not ready for the loud noise and music that came along with going to church with my grandmother *and* sitting so closely to the front row. I was so frightened that I immediately began to cry, but of course, grandma was right there to console me.

So, when the hospital had finally sent her home to spend her final moments with her family, my heart wasn't prepared to see her suffer. And as my heart was silently breaking for her, I had to act like everything was okay. But everything wasn't and pretending for so long was truly taking a toll on me. Although she was the one in pain, I felt like I was the one slowly slipping away. At the age of nine, I couldn't wrap my mind around how the one person who was always there to rescue my cousin when he was in and out of jail was the one person that the doctors couldn't save. I wanted to scream, I wanted to cry, and I wanted to be angry because I was stressed and afraid. I never saw or heard my grandmother complain about the sins of her family that weighed heavily on her weary shoulders, but she was running out of time and that meant that I was too.

After a traumatic event has occurred, children of all ages want to be reassured that things are going to be all right.

I had no idea what the death of my grandmother meant for my life considering my mother's inability to properly care for me. I was not yet in the foster care system, but I felt as if I was because I was no longer living in my home with my mother.

Children look first to their caregivers for that support. Sometimes parents are so distraught themselves that they are not aware that there are some things they should be doing to help their children cope. Very young children may not have the verbal skills to express their feelings. They express them through other means, such as play acting or drawing. Show interest in this and help them name what they are feeling. It is important that you understand every foster child is experiencing grief. While he or she may not have experienced the death of a loved one, they are likely grieving the death of their security, faith, hope, and stability.

Give honest information about the event based on the child's maturity level. Always be truthful. Tell the child that someone died rather than they "went to sleep" or "passed away" because younger children will wonder when they are coming back or be hurt that they left without saying goodbye. Death means different things to children at different ages. Young children (ages 1-5) grieve for the threat to their security, while older children (ages 6+) grieve more for the actual loss.

Don't expect the child to take care of your fears.

For example, don't keep your child home from school because you are anxious about being apart from them. Find help to cope with your own fears. Like adults, children grieve at their own pace. Respect where they are in the grieving process – there is no set timeline for grieving. Listen to them but don't force them to share; let it come naturally. One of the most important needs after a traumatic event is to talk about it – often. It may be difficult for you to hear about, or you may tire of hearing the same story, but talking is a crucial part of dealing with the impact of the disaster. Be supportive and sympathetic but avoid overreacting. Don't try to make it okay; let them express fears, thoughts, and worries.

Older children are sometimes drawn to each other for strength and support in times of tragedy. For example, allow them to spend more time than usual on the computer, texting, or talking on the phone to their friends. Don't make promises you can't keep. It is important that your child be able to count on you when there is so much else, they can't depend on or predict.

It's okay to tell your child that you don't have all the answers to their questions.

Children will not expect you to be perfect if you do not present yourself as the figure of perfection. Allow children to express all the emotions they are feeling. Children need to know that their feelings are "okay" and that lots of people have those feelings in these situations. If feelings such as anger or guilt persist for many months, professional help might be necessary to help them resolve those feelings.

No child wants to feel as if he or she is a project that needs to be fixed, repaired, or rebuilt.

Allow older children more privacy, both in physical and emotional space, if they need it to deal with their feelings. Kids who have experienced trauma don't typically ask openly for help, so if they give any clues that they have unmet needs, get help for them right away.

CHAPTER SIX

Get To Know The Child As
A Person; Not A Victim

I quickly learned that although I couldn't change the environment I lived in, I could change the environment that my thoughts were cultivated in. I could not change the situation around me, but I could change what was within me. As a young boy, I was already having conversations with myself, wondering, *Is this life? Is there truly no more to life than this?*

When I decided that I wanted better than the view from my grandparents' apartment window, there was an internal shift taking place. I longed for a better life. I had gotten a small taste of how things could be, and now the cravings of a "good life" were deeply penetrating my mental and emotional spaces. The yearning for something more was greater than my ability to continue adapting to the situations around me. You can't choose what life throws at you, but you can choose how you react. I didn't choose to be born into the environment I grew up in, but fortunately I learned that I could choose how I reacted to that environment. So, imagine, being a nine-year-old child living a life of turmoil full of disappointments, heartbreaks, stress, worry, and fear. Imagine being a child growing into a man with these unaddressed feelings and emotions.

How do you grow? How are you supposed to feel? How are you allowed to feel? How do you see one physical reality but long for something that was never supposed to be yours? How do you take those fantasies playing in your head, showing you a taste of the good life and turn them into a tangible reality? How do you go about life carrying these bricks on your back without a safe space to unpack?

I was conflicted on the inside. I was losing the internal war that was waged within me. I was hurting, I wasn't happy, and I was getting no satisfaction out of life. My head, my heart, my thoughts, my feelings, and emotions had all turned on each other and my body was their battlefield. I was losing this war and I was losing myself. The dark clouds surrounding my life challenged me to still see the light at the end of the tunnel. And although I had tunnel vision, I still couldn't see the light. I had enough hope for today but asking me to extend that same hope into my tomorrow felt like an impossible task. I was tuned in to the internal conversations that wouldn't allow me to physically cry out for help and it was beyond time for a reckoning. It was time for things to change. I knew the change I wanted and needed had to start with me. But the most important question was—how? Where would I start? Was there actually room on the journey I longed for, for someone like me?

It wasn't going to be an easy fix, and it definitely wasn't going to happen overnight! The process was long. Progression felt nonexistent. But each day I opened my eyes I had to choose to go a little further. Through the tears, the losses, the anger and frustration, and the unresolved feelings I continued to press on for the change. Why? Because, even as a young child I understood that if I stopped fighting even for just one day, then my environment would win, and I would be just another lost boy from the South Side of

Chicago who had fallen victim to the streets. And where was the greatness in that?

Soon after the death of my grandmother, I was completely blindsided by what happened next. Without warning or explanation, one day I was simply told to grab my personal items because I would no longer be living with my grandparents. I would be going to live with someone else. Remember the swimming party that had been responsible for altering my perception of life? Well, that perception was now going to be my reality because I was going to live with my cousin and her family.

I felt like a pawn in the game of life, and no one cared how it was affecting me—at least that was how it seemed at the time. My new living situation was much better than my initial one, but of course, my personal struggles soon followed me. As I attempted to get settled into my new environment, the "inner me" was having a difficult time becoming acclimated to the sudden changes. No one seemed to be aware of my unsettled feelings, thoughts, and emotions. No one seemed to be aware of or care that my internal battles, struggles, and fights with unprocessed grief and emotions were slowly overtaking me. I was hurting badly and was in desperate need of a listening ear that only my grandmother seemed to possess.

My heart was broken. I was angry, alone, confused, and the feeling of hopelessness that I had learned to embrace was, once again, right there to provide the comfort that I desperately longed for. I had so many unanswered questions. Was my grandmother's death the reason I had to leave? Was my grandfather unable or even unwilling to care for me without her?

Why hadn't my grandmother's death forced my own mother to now be a mother and take care of me? Why hadn't my dad intervened and taken me into his home like a loving parent would naturally do? What had I done to deserve this outcome? Did anyone truly love me? Why was I this unwanted plague that everyone passed around like a game of "hot potato?" I didn't understand, they didn't care if I understood, and I didn't know if I truly cared that they didn't care. The only one who had truly cared about me was now dead and my heart felt rejected and allowed me to cry so many nights, asking my grandmother why she had to leave me. I was in a better physical environment, but my comfort zone was still the rugged, untamed South Side of Chicago.

I cannot express enough the seriousness of getting to know the child as an individual, not as a product of their circumstances. I didn't feel as if anyone actually took the time to get to know me, my pains, confusions, or struggles. I was a person. Your foster child is a full human person with ideas, thoughts, and dreams that existed before they met you. You must begin engaging with the child to learn of who they are. When no one asks or seeks knowledge of who the child is, the child begins being identified simply as a number, statistic, or project. That is a horrible feeling. You are building a relationship. Just as in every relationship there has to be investment into getting to know one another.

A child or young person may feel nervous or unable to communicate with you in the way you'd like at first. This is normal – and it's all about creating relationships between your family and the foster child as well as establishing trust. Effective communication with children isn't just one-sided – ultimately, your foster child will need to communicate with you too, and that can come from listening to them when they want to talk.

It may be hard to hear what's going on in their mind, and the troubles they have encountered before entering your family – but it's important as a foster parent to listen and respond in the appropriate way. You want them to feel like they can confide in you and that you're always there to listen to them. Arguably the most important tip to building your foster relationship – make time for them. This doesn't just mean being around when they're home from school or having your dinner together. It's important to allocate time for quality bonding – this may be as simple as watching a movie together or venturing out to do an activity. Creating time for them (maybe at the same time each week to establish routine) is a great way to connect with a child and build up your foster relationship.

One of the most important aspects you'll need to achieve to establish a great foster relationship is trust. This doesn't come quickly – especially if a child or young person has had a hard past and struggle with trust issues. Trust takes time – but there are some things you can do to try and gain their trust.

Telling them something personal about you can help them to feel like they are trusted – but try not to tell them something they can use against you at a difficult time. You could also give them your trust by letting them do certain things e.g. use the computer on their own, walk the dog around the block. These small things will allow them to realize they are trusted, and then hopefully in turn, trust you too.

Of course, there can be challenging behavior that should not be positively reinforced; more attempted to be understood. But when they do demonstrate positive behavior, this should be rewarded. That way, they'll not only learn how best to control their behavior, but also see that you are willing to praise them for good behavior – and your relationship will hopefully improve. Even the smallest achievements should be praised as this will have a great impact on their confidence and self-worth. Establishing your emotional connection with your foster child can be enhanced from touch.

Children and young people will have had different experiences so this is something that your Social Worker will support you with. If appropriate, don't be afraid to give them hugs and hold their hand – letting them know you're there with physical contact is a way they will in time feel secure with you and let you in.

They may have had different experiences of physical contact in the past – and it may take them time to be comfortable; again, always involve your social worker. But letting them know you're there when they're ready is important to building up their trust. Just be aware they may not be willing to accept contact straight away – you could possibly start small such as a touch on the hand, or a hand on the shoulder and gauge how they receive it.

Whether it's their favorite dish, a large chocolate cake for the whole family to devour or quirky experimental cooking to see what you can conjure up, cooking together is a great bonding activity. It gives the foster child a sense of responsibility; the structure of following instructions from the recipe; and gives you a chance to spend time together with a relaxed activity. Children can also feel more willing to communicate in an environment where they are to the side of you as opposed to face to face – as it may be easier for them to talk.

Whether it's throwing a ball around the backyard, sitting down with a board game or imaginative play, this is a great way to bond with your foster child. Here you're not only building on your relationship, but you're also creating memories that they can hold onto and cherish when they look back on their childhood.

Exercising is a great way to not only get them moving, but also connect with your foster child. Again, this is dependent on age. If you have a young child, walks in the park, football in the back yard, or taking them swimming would be great ways to bond and get them active. If your foster child is a teenager or young adult, you could do yoga, running, countryside walks or attend gym classes such as Zumba or body conditioning classes if they're interested in fitness.

Depending on the age of the foster child, you can read to them –or get them to read to you. This not only enhances their reading skills and improve their literature, but also can be a great bonding exercise. Why not read a series of books, such as Harry Potter? That way, this will be an activity they can enjoy and something you can share together until you've finished the entire series of books.

Share something each week, or once a month, that you can both enjoy.

Really try to understand what they would like to do– this could be something as simple as painting or drawing, or maybe something a little more adventurous like rock-climbing or ice skating. This would depend on the age of your foster child – it's easier to share a hobby with a teenager or young adult, so this would be

a creative way to connect with a teenage foster daughter
or son.

CHAPTER SEVEN

Lower Your Expectancies, not Your Tolerance.

Upon graduating from the eighth grade, I had no clear plan in sight other than reaching out to a family friend who worked for Percy L. Julian High School in hopes of continuing my education. When I was accepted the day before school started, I was grateful because I honestly had no "Plan B." This was it for me. It didn't take long for me to realize that Julian was filled with an array of distractions, to say the least.

More than one-thousand students attended the school, 99.8% were African American while the other .2% was Hispanic and many of the students were from low-income families in the surrounding neighborhoods. As a result, you can imagine how "at home" I felt when my academic surroundings literally mimicked the ghetto that I had once called home.

Though I was attending school for an education, I quickly learned that I would have to resort to some of my street tactics as a means of survival and I also needed to become sociable enough to establish a few key relationships. The halls were filled with people, some who had been friends since birth, others who I had attended elementary school with, as well as a few cliques. I understood that if I was going to survive in this culture for the next four years, the friends and relationships I made needed to be significant.

So, I started with the upperclassmen. My brother had graduated the year prior to my enrollment so I felt like he probably had enough clout as a "B-Boy" that as his little brother, I would be okay. A B-Boy was slang for someone who was heavily involved in hip hop culture, and these guys were very well known throughout my high school. I began to build relationships with several of the B-Boys by stepping out of my comfort zone and introducing myself, sparking random conversations with them until it was apparent that my presence wasn't going to be an issue.

You know what they say, *"if it ain't broke, don't fix it,"* so I used this same process with different groups and individuals throughout the school and it worked in my favor. The issue with making friends with so many people is you are also influenced by so many people. Whether those influences are positive or negative may not always be initially apparent, but somehow, you will be influenced. I was being pulled in so many different directions and my desire to say "no" was sometimes non-existent.

I remember being introduced to weed and initially I only smoked it occasionally. It soon turned into almost an addiction, to the point that I was willing to lie my way out of obligations for the sake of getting high. I remember going to a basketball scrimmage and I had come up with what I thought was a foolproof plan to tell my coach that I was ill so he would allow me to sit on the bench. To my surprise, everyone on my team including my coach knew that I was high, and the coach refused to allow me to sit out. He rode me so hard that I can still hear him yelling, "hustle," even today.

When we become so attached to our own ideas about how something "should" be, or how a child "should" behave, we can make the caretaking of a foster child harder than it has to be. Of course, we parents are human, and we feel strangely comfortable with our "shoulds" – so much of our own lives are all too often dictated by expectations set for us from the outside world. Our challenge is to shift our expectations from what we thought it "should" be like to raise our children, to accept things for how they are. We must establish expectations that are appropriate to our current circumstances.

Adjusting your expectations is not to be confused with settling for "less," or "lowering" your standards for your foster child.

You have every reason to set high expectations for the kids. What's different, here, is that I am encouraging you to set your expectations in the context of truly accepting your child for who they are, not who you want them to be. That is the most important desire we as adults even desire for ourselves. Make sure you're communicating clearly with your child, making sure she or he understands directions and what you do expect.

As a foster parent, you must be willing to change how you're looking at things in order to help your complex child reach an adulthood of independence and fulfillment.

If your foster child were in a wheelchair, you wouldn't put him at the bottom of a flight of stairs and tell him to run on up to the top. If you wanted him to reach the top, you'd certainly expect that he would have to find another method to get there—perhaps using his arms to pull himself up, or maybe even setting up an elaborate pulley system. You'd probably expect it to take longer, and his achievement at the top would be all the greater, of course, for his challenge and struggle on the journey. You'd probably celebrate it more heartily than you would a child who could just run on up the stairs.

Sometimes we forget to take the "Disability" perspective with foster kids. But it's important, and it shows up in every aspect of their life. Take the emotional realm, for example. These kids are not generally as mature as their same-aged peers, and they're not as skilled at managing their emotions. It is highly offensive to anyone to assume they should have the same standards, expectations, goals, and values as you.

When we presume that they "should" be able to behave in a certain way – that they "should" be old enough to know better – we must make sure that we are not telling them to hop out of the wheelchair and run on up the stairs. Let go of how people see you as a foster parent. You're serving the child, not public opinion.

Focus on the child, instead of worrying about how things might look to others who may not have the same empathy, purpose, or heart as you. Without treating them as a younger child, expect your foster child to behave about 3-5 years younger than his/her same aged peers in some areas. Choose your battles, being deliberate about when you want to pursue an issue, and when it's okay to let something slide. No adult or child can maintain a positive self-image with constant critique.

A little over halfway through my freshman year of high school, I went back to live with my mother. My uncle would become so frustrated with me that he would often threaten to send me back to her as a form of punishment. He had no clue that his threats were a welcomed form of relief for me because if I was sent back to live with my mother, then at least I wouldn't have to deal with him any longer.

My grandfather still lived in the same apartment that I had once called home, but my mother had moved about a mile away. My grandfather was aging and now that I was older, I knew he could use my help. Being home felt just as scary as it felt comfortable because although nothing about the environment had changed, I was no longer a naive little boy blinded to the world around me.

I didn't have to go looking for trouble because if I wasn't cautious, trouble would just find me. After several months while living with my grandfather he thought it best for me to go stay with my mom because his apartment no longer had running water. I completely understood his logic, but I was very hesitant to leave because of my concern for him and because this move would be the first time that I had lived with my mom since I was about two years old. Nevertheless, I obeyed his request. I'll never forget the day I left my grandfather's apartment with a new awareness. I had read in the newspaper that 1 out of every 4 black males from my community would either be dead or in jail between the ages of 18-21.

It was as if time had literally stopped, and for the first time in years I had something else to live for. I wasn't sure where they'd gotten their information from, but I knew I didn't want to be another statistic. I had something to prove. I didn't have anyone in my corner coaching me through life. I didn't have anyone to show me how to beat the odds, but I had a new motivation to be better than my environment said I was supposed to be.

CHAPTER EIGHT

Room to Breathe

I had never struggled with feelings of anger prior to living with my aunt's family, but not long after I began to develop a short fuse. I typically didn't have "blow ups" at school or in my day-to-day relationships with people. My anger seemed to be triggered in an environment that was supposed to be good for me but was actually emotionally difficult for me.

The source of my anger stemmed from the pain I felt as a result of being removed from the only family I had ever known. In so many ways, I was blaming my aunt and her family for what was happening to me. At the time, my anger wouldn't allow me to see that they were only trying to help me. Yet their help would have never been good enough because I was hurting and as far as I was concerned, these people were partially responsible for my pain, so I placed an emotional barrier between us.

I cannot reiterate the seriousness of conducting a moral and emotional inventory of yourself prior to becoming the foster parent or kinship guardian to a child who has experienced trauma. You cannot just take the approach to assume that as long as your home is better than the child's past home that all is well. Security is so much deeper than that.

You are saying that you have the ability to master adjustments yourself. The responsibility is not solely on the child who just had the rug snatched from beneath them. If you are going to serve children in this fashion, you should be willing and able to adjust to meet the needs, healthy norms, and reasonable expectations of the child as well. You're the conscious adult with a full understanding of the severity of foster care. The more adjusting you are willing to do, the more patience you can offer to the child while he or she adjusts as well.

You will do yourself and the child a great service by giving everyone room to breathe. You will need your quiet moments as well as the child. You will need a support system. The only people who truly understand what you're going through are other foster parents or caretakers in similar situations.

Finding a support network is invaluable—it will save your life. I know because it saved mine.

When you connect with other foster parents, you'll have people who can answer questions and offer insight into child behaviors or challenges you might be having with a child's birth parent.

You'll have friends who won't blink when your foster child throws the most epic tantrum or when you have a baby who won't stop screaming. They know because they've been there—in fact, they're probably there right now.

When you're starting out, make the effort to attend the training sessions offered by your agency. You'll learn about things like caring for kids with special needs, court proceedings for foster children and self-care for foster families and—perhaps more importantly—you'll connect with other foster parents. Attend special events offered by your agency and get to know other families. You'll need the support and friendship, so don't be afraid to seek it out.

Now in high school, my life still had many challenges and issues that needed to be resolved. My displays of anger involved pacing and punching walls, but now I had hope and hope was my personal plot twist! Let's dive a little deeper into some of these feelings and how we can begin to work through and past them.

Have you ever blown up a balloon? As the balloon fills with air, it continues to expand, and if you continue to blow the balloon beyond its capacity to expand then it bursts. Why? Because the pressure was greater than the balloon had room to expand. Anger operates in a similar manner. I'm not saying that your anger isn't justified. I'm saying that if you don't release it and get rid of it then it will begin to come out in unexpected ways. For me it was going a few rounds with the wall. For you it might be snapping on someone who doesn't deserve it. It may be sleepless nights or the inability to find peace. Haven't you carried it around long enough? It's time to release it and let it go.

When I took my time to breathe, I found calmness in drawing. Several years later, I still find it incredible how I discovered drawing as a way to manage my anger. I was never an artist by any means. I was actually the kid in art class in awe of other people's work and totally embarrassed by my own. One day I saw a picture in a coloring book that I would have normally traced because I couldn't draw anything of style from my own imagination. But on this day I challenged myself to try. It was tough in the beginning, but I enjoyed the challenge. Initially it was foreign and uncomfortable, but I noticed when I would become angry or upset, instead of punching holes in the wall, I would allow my imagination to run free.

Have you ever worked out? I mean like truly worked out and pushed yourself beyond what you thought you were capable of doing? What do you think about as you're coaching yourself to keep going? Are you feeling sorry for yourself? Are you determined to quit because you're feeling hopeless? Maybe, but not usually. Often, all of the tension and stress you've found yourself carrying around is now being released through the burning you feel seeping into your muscles and ligaments. Exercising when angry helped me to calm down and move forward in a positive way. You don't have time to be angry when you're focused on feeling the burn. Setting aside a workout room or area in the home, garage, or backyard can be a great outlet for the foster child and you also.

As a young man my self-worth was very low and essentially non-existent. I was unable to see myself as important because if my own mother, the woman who had carried and birthed me, didn't want me then how could I have worth or value? As I lived with these negative feelings on a daily basis, they began to take root in my mind in almost an all-consuming way. So, I went back to thinking about my "good thing," my grandmother.

As I would think of her, so many pleasant things would cross my mind. I would think about how much she loved me. Thinking about her love for me reminded me of my "why," and as a result, I would think about the words she would frequently say to me when she was still alive. "Son, it's okay." "You are precious and wonderfully made." "You were created and hand-picked by God to do something amazing; and you're handsome, smart, and intelligent."

As I imagined her speaking these words to me, the way I viewed myself began to change. I began to hold my head high. I stood and walked with my chest out, and I walked with my shoulders back as I began to echo these words daily to myself. "I am loved. I am somebody. I'm priceless because I'm one of a kind. I do have value and worth. My present circumstances and situations will not dictate or determine my value. As long as I'm alive there is meaning for my life. My mother's mistake does not mean that I was or am a mistake."

CHAPTER NINE

The Power of Acceptance

The power of acceptance is a gift that I pray you can accept for the success of your foster parenting journey. I also pray that you can share your learning of this power with the foster child that you so dearly wish to empower. Acceptance isn't passive. It doesn't mean that you're resigned to a life of unhappiness, broken relationships, or just putting up with things. Accepting things as they are is a beautiful starting point that opens possibilities you may have never considered.

As a misplaced child, I moved a total of four times within a six-year span. Having my own bedroom was rare occurrence. Being the new kid in school was my social norm and sleeping on a couch or an air mattress in a makeshift bedroom was everyday living for me.

Living in my aunt's office space with only a sink to bathe in as a preteen boy definitely took its toll on me. Yes, I was grateful for a roof over my head and that all of my basic necessities were being provided for, but something was wrong with this picture. As a result of my situation, over time I began to become very unhappy in a way that I had never experienced. I felt like nothing was right in my life; like the walls were closing in on me and all that was left was me. Living a life of struggle was common to me. Not having all the things that I wanted was normal. But the thoughts that tormented my mind was a different story. The vigor I had for life was gone. Even my level of optimism seemed to be non-existent. I was tired, fatigued, dejected, and downright exhausted. I had no more fight left in me, and depression had become the only version of me that felt "right."

At night when I would lay down for bed, the movie trailer of my life would play out over and over in my mind. This trailer only showed my inadequacies and at the end of each clip was nothing but doom and gloom—as if it were the latest preview for a sad movie. I felt so defeated and worthless as I would lie awake on my air mattress trying to figure out where my life was truly headed if it even had a sense of direction at all. Remember when I said your thoughts begin to take on lives of their own? I know from experience because the constant negative thoughts that were consuming me ultimately opened the door for me to contemplate suicide.

I had heard of people dying by or attempting suicide but now I was one of those people having such thoughts. I would reassure myself that when it was finally time to "do it," I would finish the task. I wouldn't be another "failed" statistic because no one cared if I was alive or dead anyway. My thoughts were so loud that I no longer knew what silence was. I was alone, I was worthless, I was not valued or wanted, and when the time was right, I even knew the method of how I would take my own life. I would permanently silence my tormented mind.

The voices in my head would ask me "when?" and my answer was always the same, "tomorrow." Tomorrow came and went and tomorrow was never the day. One day, as I was wallowing in my own despair, my grandmother came to mind. I was reminded that she had been my reason for living and I still had yet to make her proud. If I ended my life, then how would I ever make her proud? I had to push forward, and I had to do it for her! I had to finally sit in the space of understanding that my grandmother was gone, and my mother was not the mother I wanted her to be. No matter how much I felt my mother should be someone else, she was not.

Not accepting things as they are is a fight against reality.

It's kind of crazy, really. Say that someone said something hurtful to you. You can wish they hadn't said it forever, but the fact remains the same—they said what they said. Say you did something you regret. You can wish you hadn't done it, which could keep you stuck for a long time, but here's the truth—you did what you did.

The problem with wishful thinking, wanting things to be different than they are, is that it's agitating. It resists what's real and keeps you ruminating and analyzing to try to make sense of it so that you feel better. But it doesn't work, and it won't bring you happiness. No matter how much you may desire a closer relationship with your foster child, you have to accept the reality. Just as important as it is for the child to accept the present circumstances, the child should not feel pressured because of your inability to accept that he or she may never be the child you imagined them to be. Acceptance is the opposite of avoidance or denial. It's a full-hearted, all-encompassing, enthusiastic and courageous "Yes" to things as they are. It is open, welcoming, and ultimately freeing—like a breath of fresh air.

Acceptance is taking an honest look at things as they are right now. You let go of judging or interpreting the acts of the child. You don't need to add the layer of feeling like a failure or victim because of the situation. Rather than turning away from what is, you turn toward it and receive what's there with great compassion and understanding.

One of the key survival tactics in the hood is keeping your ear to the streets. I remember staring out of the window at my grandfather's apartment and hearing the words, "there he is! Get him!" immediately followed by a series of gunshots. Not long after the gunshots rang out, there were police lights and sirens that filled the Southside city streets. As I watched the police search a few handcuffed men, I heard one of the men yell "get my face off of the hood of this hot car!" My grandfather then yelled for me to stop being nosey, but I was keeping my ear to the streets.

Most people in my neighborhood ran in cliques; you rarely saw anyone rolling alone, so because I preferred to roll alone the window of our second-floor apartment was my spot. It was my way of still knowing what was going on outside without having to involve myself in the chaos.

I am a firm believer that you can learn from someone else's experiences just as well as you can learn from your own. I prefer this approach because it prevents me from having to learn a specific lesson the hard way. The lesson I was learning from my apartment window was that most of the guys in the neighborhood were up to no good, and birds of a feather flock together.

So, typically if you saw one man running you soon saw his clique not too far behind. If the saying is true, "you're only as good as the company you keep," then wisdom says not to associate myself with these individuals. Right? So, to keep my own nose clean, it meant keeping to myself and rolling solo. I'll admit, at times I felt lonely but as I reminded myself that I had greater goals than becoming the latest statistic handcuffed to the hood of the police car, it became easier to walk alone. I was always observing, analyzing, and learning the world around me. I was slow to speak but quick to watch and listen. My only chance of survival was wholeheartedly accepting who I was, who I was not, and where I was. I was not like everyone else. Until we can accept the reality around us, we can never succeed as caretakers to children in need or ourselves.

The inability to accept reality will cause you to second guess absolutely everything you come up against—every decision you've ever made and every thought you may be wrestling with. But if you spend your entire life second guessing every waking moment, when do you ever find the chance to actually live? It's time to take life moment by moment and make the best of each day we're given. There are so many people who have died trying to survive what you've overcome. There are so many people who criticize your decisions but who would have never been strong enough to live with the consequences of choosing differently.

I remember walking home from school one day and the streetlights were out. If you know anything at all about the hood, then you also know that the streetlights mean a variety of different things. In this situation it meant I was walking into potential danger. As I cautiously walked down the street, trying to be vigilant of my dark surroundings, I heard a male voice ask from behind a parked car on the opposite side of the street, "who are you?" Fear immediately rose up inside of me because not only could I not see his face, but remember, I had plans to make it out of the ghetto on my own terms and not in a body bag.

As I froze with fear, another male voice quickly came to my defense and said, "I know him, he's good." Naturally, I began to think about the millions of ways my situation could have turned out. What if I had decided not to stop for a snack on my walk home from school? What if I would have run when I heard the first man's voice? What if I would have taken another route?

Shortly after arriving home, there was a knock at the door. This was a surprise to me because I didn't typically have company. The knock at the door was from the second man behind the car. There had been a gang war that day while I was at school and the gang in my neighborhood had made the decision to do bodily harm to anyone "out of place." He wanted to offer me a place in his gang making lots of money.

This offer was appealing to me because I didn't have money, and I didn't come from money. So, to have more than the bus tokens that often lined my pockets was truly something worth considering.

I knew I could never do anything illegal though because seeing my cousin in and out of jail my entire childhood had shown me that I truly wasn't made for that life, and after I nervously declined his offer, he left without confrontation.

Once you give yourself the gift of acceptance, you'll free yourself from second guessing your success as a foster parent.

Whenever I thought of my grandmother, it had a unique way of calming me down and giving me a sense of peace. I realized that I had not yet properly grieved her death or the idea of her truly being gone. I was hurting but I couldn't heal if I kept avoiding the process of accepting the reality surrounding her passing. She was physically gone but she still lived within me, and as I began to accept this, I also learned to allow myself to be at peace with her physical absence.

It was time to add another layer to my level of my healing, and that was acceptance. I allowed my "good thing" to fuel my drive for more so I wouldn't become stagnant. Acceptance doesn't mean we're supposed to be still and stop moving forward. I then gave myself permission to feel whatever I needed to feel about a situation, but I didn't allow it to be an excuse as to why I couldn't move on. I woke up every day and decided that today I would be better than I was yesterday. I made the choice to be grateful even on those days when I wanted to be angry.

Although I truly loved my mom, the thought of forgiving her was so foreign to me, but I was evolving spiritually, mentally, and emotionally. So, I knew that my further development would be directly linked to my ability to forgive her. I had so many feelings of hurt, neglect, and anger toward her and they were beginning to be almost impossible to control. One minute I would be okay, and the next I was lashing out simply because I had heard the sound of her voice.

I tried shaking it off, but it took an honest conversation with myself to understand that my mother had hurt me and I was allowed to feel it. But I had to face it and address it to actually heal from it. I was holding so many questions inside because I couldn't bring myself to actually allow her to answer them. I was convinced that she "owed" me answers, but I was also convinced that there was nothing she could say to me that I didn't already know, so I held them all inside. I had spent so much time being angry with her, that I never took the time to see how desperately she tried to make amends by just being there for her children.

She had spent most of my childhood either using drugs or drinking, but when I lived with her, she never failed to make sure we had food on the table. She didn't have much but she went out of her way to acknowledge our birthdays and other important days. As I began to shift my attention to her more positive attributes, I also began to forgive her for being an imperfect human, trying to carry the weight of the consequences of her own actions.

Shortly after learning to forgive my mother, my life took two unexpected turns. Due to a complaint, my mother was invested by the Department of Children and Family Services of Illinois. My mother was accused of child neglect after drugs were found in my newborn sister. And it was at this very moment that I became a ward of the State of Illinois. I was officially placed in the foster care system.

During this time my grandfather was moving out of the only real home I had ever known. Since he was considered close to kin the state allowed me to live with him. This transition came with a laundry list of concerns and fears, but my grandfather handled everything with poise and grace as he always had, and as a result, I followed his lead.

Secondly, I was presented with an incredible opportunity to attend Chicago High School for Agricultural Sciences. My new school was a culture shock. There were people from diverse backgrounds. There were no aggressive security guards roaming the halls. Students seemed to take their education seriously and I felt like my safety was an actual priority. I was actually pursuing the life I had promised myself, and everything was going well until my grandfather was diagnosed with lung cancer at the start of the summer following my junior year of high school. My entire summer was spent basically living alone as my grandfather spent most of his days at the hospital.

His health and strength quickly deteriorated, and the tone of his voice soon began to follow. He more often than not sounded hoarse and raspy, but one day as he lay in his hospital bed he handed me a check for the rent and groceries. I was stunned. His physical appearance was anything but okay, but mentally he had not forgotten about keeping a roof over my head and food in my belly. I asked him why he was concerned about paying bills when his current situation would allow him to neglect it for a while and his response to me was, "son, always take care of your responsibilities; no matter what."

I left the hospital to pay the rent and put food in the house, but I couldn't stop thinking about what had just happened. Even as my grandfather was dying, he was determined to continue making an honest man out of me yet. A few weeks later, my family received a call that he had a few days left to live and if we wanted to say our final goodbyes, now was the time to do it. I allowed my family to have their time with him and when it was my turn, I went in alone. I reached for his hand as he lay there almost unresponsive, and I could tell that he was tired in ways that didn't require sleeping. As I sat with the reality of this, I had an overwhelming sense of peace and courage. I no longer wanted to see him suffer for the sake of holding on for me. I bent down to his ear and said "grandfather, it's okay. I'll be alright. Go and be at peace." I saw his eyes flicker in an attempt to open, but he was too weak to open them, and this was my sign that he had heard me. I stood up and walked out of his room, grateful that I had the opportunity to talk to him one last time. Within an hour, he was gone.

CHAPTER TEN

Be Grateful

After my grandfather passed away, I was forced to face the reality that everything I had done up until that point was to make my grandmother proud from heaven and to make my grandfather proud enough to show up for my events. Events like prom, graduation, beating the odds, and just choosing life had all been planned with the thought in mind that he would be around to witness them. My heart was in so many pieces and I was in so much pain, and the pain had me on my knees.

On the day of my grandfather's funeral, I realized I wasn't alone. A few of my closest classmates showed up and my home economics teacher Mrs. Lane also attended. I had such a sense of peace and comfort that surpassed even my own understanding. When it was time for me to get up and speak, I had no clue what I was supposed to say, but I knew I had to say something about my grandfather because he was so much more than a grandparent; he was like my father. As I stood behind the microphone and looked into the eyes of those who were in attendance, I was suddenly overtaken with emotion as I struggled to speak the words that my mind had formed. Tears began to spill out of my eyes. I tried to speak but I couldn't. I tried to be strong and fight the emotions, but it was no use. As I stood on the pulpit fighting my feelings, I felt the hand of the pastor consoling me as he said, "it's okay, take your time son."

Suddenly I heard my grandfather's words replaying in my mind, reminding me of the importance of always handling my responsibilities which also meant standing tall during inconvenient or uncomfortable times and situations. Two months later, I was welcomed into the home of a childhood friend and for the first time since I had been alive, I had stability and I lived in a neighborhood that offered me safety and security. I absolutely loved it! I was motivated and focused. I was going to finish my senior year strong! I had to do it for my grandmother, the one who loved me when I didn't think anyone else did. I had to do it for those who said that one out of four black males from my community would end up in jail or dead by age eighteen. I had to do it for my grandfather, because at his weakest state he was still mindful of taking care of his responsibilities no matter what. I had to do it for me, because I had come so far and been through so much that quitting wasn't an option.

I'll never forget my senior year when I was putting my books in my locker. A feeling that I had never felt before hit me like a ton of bricks and I was no match for the uncontrollable need to cry. As I let out this cry from the depths of my soul and my classmates surrounded me, I realized I had been strong for so long that I was never given permission to be "human."

I had been through so many things, yet I had never taken the time to mourn the pieces of me I had lost during my frequent transitions. I had spent my last two-and-a-half years drowning in unprocessed emotions and I was never allowed the opportunity to release them. That day in the hallway of my high school would be the day it happened. That day had to be the best day of my life because it gave me the necessary room to push forward with tunnel vision right across the graduation stage. I had so much more support than I had allowed myself to realize. It was perfect. My girlfriend was present, my parents were both present, and so were my brothers. Although my grandparents weren't physically present, I knew they were always there with me, pushing and motivating me to keep going.

All of my sacrifices and hard work had paid off! Who would have thought that this traumatized kid from the ghetto in the Southside of Chicago would have been caught walking across the graduation stage? Every day I was faced with something different. There was always another decision, there was always another choice, there was always another opportunity; and there was always my determination to be better than the article in the Chicago Sun Times said I was supposed to be. Not only did I graduate from high school on time without being held back or dropping out due to my circumstances, but I also enrolled in Alabama A&M University. I was a first-generation college student! I graduated from high school. I lived to see age eighteen. I never joined a gang. I never participated in any illegal activities in pursuit of financial gain like selling drugs. I've never been to jail. And last but not least, I made it out of Chicago alive. I beat the odds that were stacked against me and all I could say was, "Grandma this is for you! Grandfather, I made it!"

The journey of healing starts the minute you no longer are consumed by your exterior environment and you begin to focus and pay attention to your internal environment.

Underneath all of the debris of hurt, disappointment, regrets, low self-esteem, depression, rejection, abuse, and addiction is a beautiful flower. That flower is waiting to break through all of the trauma that has tried to stunt its growth. Regardless of how toxic your environment is, there is hope and the possibility of overcoming it from the inside out.

The beautiful thing about forgiveness is the freedom it offers you in exchange. Forgiving someone for hurting you doesn't mean the hurt they've caused you wasn't valid or non-existent; it simply means you've decided to allow yourself the peace that comes along with not having to carry around the pain and hurt every day. If you never receive an apology, does the world stop turning and does the sun stop rising and setting to mark a new day? Absolutely not, so why then should you allow your life to become so wrapped up in receiving an apology that you become stuck? Forgiveness is a choice; sometimes you have to wake up every day determined to move on a little further past the trauma today than you did yesterday. Do it! The peace you gain in return far outweighs the need to continue holding a grudge.

I have shared with you my story as a testament to the difference that people just like you have the ability to make in the life of a child. I would not be here if it were not for people like yourself who's hearts had been graced by the touch of God.

My mother eventually died due to complications from her many years of addiction. Less than a week later my brother died also. I returned home a minister and performed the eulogy for them both in a dual funeral. After a lifetime of health issues due to my mother's drug use while pregnant with her, my sister died as well. I found my peace, my purpose, and my power in my ability to be grateful.

The word "grateful" has the power to shift your entire paradigm, which is simply the way you look at or think about something. Being grateful was the first principle that I began to live by to better cope with the feelings and negative emotions that were brewing inside of me as I embarked on my initial journey of healing and growth.

With all of the negative things that were happening in my life, hopelessness was a byproduct of my feelings and emotions. It's how I perceived the things that were happening to me and around me. We often hear about how powerful our words are but not enough is said about the power of our own thoughts.

If your mind is consistently filled with negative thoughts and emotions, then where is there room for positivity to be cultivated and then spoken? I'm sure we've all heard the phrase, "for every action there is a reaction." So, if your thoughts are negative then naturally so are your words, right? If you're thinking negative thoughts all day, how do you think you will feel at the end of the day? Now let's flip it. If you think positive thoughts all day, how do you think you'll realistically begin to feel at the end of the day?

As I was going through my own trials, I couldn't manifest any positive thoughts because I had allowed hopelessness to become who I was as a result of my negative thoughts. It's not always as simple as it sounds, but regardless of what's going on around us, we still hold the power to decide how we're going to respond to and think about these things. As I began to heal, grow, and change my personal perspective I also began to use the words like "so called" to describe negative situations.

Why? Because, even in those "unchangeable" moments, it was still about my perspective. It's like the glass half empty or glass half full analogy—whether your glass is half empty or half full is contingent upon your own perspective of the glass and the contents in it. My life was miserable and unhappy because I had chosen to allow what I saw around me to determine how I saw the world around me. You're probably wondering how I can say that I chose something that I didn't have any control over, right? That's a logical question, and here is the answer—although I couldn't technically choose my surroundings and environment, I still had the ability to decide my own perspective regarding those things.

I could have decided to become bitter and angry. I could have used my situation as a crutch to live a less than grateful life...OR I could choose to take what I saw on a daily basis and use it as motivation to "level up" and get out of that hopeless environment.

The "inner me" was a toxic landfill. I was filled with a countless number of negative thoughts and feelings. I felt rejected, angry, fear, worry, misunderstood, abandoned, blame, alone, lonely, not valuable, and even depressed. As a result, my change didn't happen overnight; it was an uphill battle with seemingly no end in sight. It was incredibly difficult! Many nights I cried myself to sleep because my process was overwhelming and often frustrating. I hated the way I had grown to feel, and I so badly wanted to change it, so I did. Here is how I did it—when I found myself slipping into a negative mindset, I would choose to think about something positive. It worked! It's amazing how many positive things you overlook when you aren't looking for reasons to notice them.

As I identified these positive reasons to be grateful, I also began to realize that my life wasn't really all that bad. This was an excellent start, but it wasn't enough. I needed more. So, I then decided to take things a step further. I challenged myself to identify the positive things in my life that meant the most to me; the things I was most grateful for.

There was one thing or person that truly stood out and if you've read this far then I'm sure you know that one good thing for me was my grandmother. Why? Because although she was no longer alive, I still found myself consumed by a euphoria of good and happy thoughts, feelings, and emotions whenever I thought about her. So I decided that my grandmother would be the center of my daily gratitude.

What I want you to do is to identify at least one thing that you're grateful for above everything else. If you're able to identify several things then that's great, and if you can only identify one thing or a few, then that's okay too.

This will be the catalyst to infuse your thoughts and emotions with positive energy. I realized that thinking about my grandmother (my good thing) was a pivotal role in chasing those dark clouds in my mind away. I thought about her in an almost obsessive way because I understood that thinking negatively had gotten me to a place of gloom, sorrow, and misery. I couldn't afford to stay in that place anymore.

My "good thing" had become my secret weapon, tucked away in the deepest corners of my mind and in my most intimate thoughts. It was the foundation for my change of heart in my pursuit of a greater life and way of thinking, living, and being. My grandmother's prayers kept me safe as I was going through my life navigating through the dangerous streets of Chicago, but just knowing her saved my life and pushed me to become a better person and ultimately a better man. A man that was ready to live a life worth living.

The words "be grateful" was the tool I needed and used to help positively alter my internal environment. Though I wasn't able to control my external environment, I was now in full control of my internal environment. I was the boss of me and not my circumstances, situations, or the evil words someone might have said to or spoken over me. It was an everyday process. It was a journey and it's a process that I still use today. As you continue to serve the children who need your love, compassion, and tolerance, I dare you to focus on your ability to be grateful. What greater honor than that of serving the soul of a child?

I am Mr. BE GRATEFUL and I thank you for taking this journey with me. I pray that my story and my strategies may give you the hope and tools you need to press on another day. From all the children of the foster care systems worldwide, thank you. God Bless.

THE END

DEDICATIONS

To my amazing grandparents who shouldered the weight of the entire family; two people who I viewed as my mom and dad. What I will always remember about my grandparents is not so much what they said, but how they lived their lives. They are my real life superheroes.

This book is dedicated to my mom who is no longer with us and to my dad. If it wasn't for them I wouldn't be here today and for that I'm so grateful. Through their imperfections I've learned what it means to persevere and never give up.
I'm honored to be their son.

To my spiritual parents who willingly sacrifice each and every day for the sake of the gospel. Your impact in my life is priceless.

DEDICATIONS

To all of the individuals who have ever spoken encouraging words to me and shared words of wisdom. To the various individuals who opened up their homes and hearts to me.

To my caseworker Ms. Heard while I was in the foster care system. Your consistent support over those years was priceless and helped me more than you will ever know.

To my soulmate, my angel, my good thing, my wife; you are my dream come true. And to my four boys Isaac, Levi, Caleb, and Judah. As you all grow and mature as men I hope that you will find comfort, strength, inspiration, and wisdom from something shared in this book and the example I've set before you.

DEDICATIONS

To you the survivor; through all of the heartbreak and disappointment you are still here. I wrote this for you with the hopes that it will stir up and ignite the greatness that is within you.

Last but not least, to my Lord and Savior Jesus Christ. Thank you for always being a present help in my time of need.

CPSIA information can be obtained
at www.ICGtesting.com
Printed in the USA
BVHW050013220123
656769BV00006B/65